598.78
KIT   Kite, Lorien

            Hornbills

DATE DUE

JA 11 '12 R 2 4 '06			
AP 1 0 '12			
SE 1 6 '14			
AP - 6 '			
SEP 1 2 201			

Nature's Children

HORNBILLS

Lorien Kite

GROLIER
EDUCATIONAL

FACTS IN BRIEF

Classification of Hornbills

Class:	*Aves* (birds)
Order:	*Coraciiformes*
Suborder:	*Bucerotiformes* (hornbills)
Genus:	There are nine genera of hornbills.
Species:	There are 54 species of hornbills.

World distribution.   Africa, India, and Southeast Asia.

Habitat.   Tropical forest and savanna.

Distinctive physical characteristics.   Very large, horn-shaped beak, often capped with a horny growth called a casque; dark plumage with white, cream, or yellow markings on the tail, wings, and throat; short, broad, rounded wings.

Habits.   Live in pairs, small family groups, or large flocks. Very noisy, with booming voices and loud wing beats. Nest in tree holes, which the female seals up, leaving a narrow slit just wide enough for her beak to poke through.

Diet.   Fruit, insects, snakes, and small birds and mammals.

© 1999 Brown Partworks Limited
Printed and bound in U.S.A.
Editor: James Kinchen
Designer: Tim Brown

Published by:

GROLIER
EDUCATIONAL

Sherman Turnpike, Danbury,
Connecticut 06816

Library of Congress Cataloging-in-Publishing Data
Hornbills.
     p. cm. -- (Nature's children. Set 6)
     ISBN 0-7172-9359-9 (alk. paper) -- ISBN 0-7172-9351-3 (set)
     1. Hornbills--Juvenile Literature. [1. Hornbills.] I. Grolier Educational (Firm) II. Series.
QL696.C729K58 1999
598.7'8—dc21   98-33413

Contents

As the sun sets over the forest, a hornbill flies across the darkening sky. Large and with an oversized beak and a long, trailing tail, its outline is clearly recognizable, even from a distance. Hornbills are so striking that in many parts of Africa and Asia they are seen as sacred birds.

Hornbills are also extremely noisy. Their booming calls can carry for miles. They have the loudest wing beats of any bird, and they chuff like steam locomotives as they fly. A large flock sounds like a distant thunderstorm!

Hornbills are smart and have many cunning tricks for finding food. Their unique nesting habits have made them into a symbol of loving marriage. Read on to learn all about this fascinating family of birds.

This helmeted hornbill makes a striking silhouette against the sky.

Meet the Hornbills

Hornbills come in many shapes and sizes. There are over 50 species, which range from around 15 inches (40 centimeters) to more than five feet (one and a half meters) in length.

Most hornbills are tree birds. They have strong feet for perching and are good at hopping from branch to branch. The turkey-sized ground hornbills of Africa are the heavyweights of the family and are the only hornbills that spend most of their time on the ground. They walk rather than hop and have longer legs than the tree-dwelling types.

Hornbills have glossy coats of black, brown, or gray feathers, often with patches of white, cream, or yellow on their tails, wings, and throats. Some species have brightly colored patches of bare skin around their eyes and necks.

"What are you staring at?" The bright red throat of an African ground hornbill attracts attention.

Hornbill Territory

Hornbills are found in Africa, India, and Southeast Asia. Most species live in tropical rain forests, where it is warm and wet all year round, and the trees can grow as tall as 20-story buildings. Tropical rain forests are very rich in life. They are home to over half of the world's plant and animal species.

In Africa there are many hornbills living in much drier habitats. These places range from dry woodlands to sun-baked savannas—vast plains of swaying grass scattered with thorn bushes and small, stunted trees. This is the home of the African ground hornbills.

The African ground hornbill shares its savanna home with many animals, including gazelles such as this one.

Shock Absorber

Hornbills get their names from their huge, horn-shaped beaks. Those of the biggest hornbills can grow to more than one foot (30 centimeters) in length. The beaks of most hornbills are capped by a strange, horny growth that looks like a ridge, helmet, or horn. On some species it is bigger than the beak itself!

Experts think that this growth, called a casque, works as a kind of shock absorber. Hornbills snap their jaws with such force that without a casque they might shatter their beaks. In all but one species of hornbill the casque is hollow, so it is not as heavy as it looks. It is connected to the mouth by narrow openings. Because of this scientists think that the casque may also work like a built-in musical instrument, giving the hornbill a loud voice that can carry over a great distance.

A rhinoceros hornbill's casque looks a heavy weight to carry—but in fact it is very light.

There for the Picking

If you like fruit, you would love life in a rain forest. Plenty of rain and sunshine mean that the trees can bear fruit at any time of the year. There are hundreds of different types of fruits. However, you have to be a good climber to eat them. Most grow 120 to 150 feet (35 to 45 meters) above the ground. Here the trees spread their branches to form a leafy roof called the forest canopy.

Rainforest hornbills eat mainly fruit. Sweet, juicy figs are their favorite. Hornbills prefer juicy fruits—they never drink so have to get all of their water from their food.

Unlike people, hornbills swallow the fruits that they find whole, seeds and all. Once they have digested the flesh, they cough up the seeds and spit them out. This can happen when the hornbill is many miles from the fruit-bearing tree. This is how hornbills help the forest in return for their meals—some of the seeds they spit out will grow into more fruit-bearing trees.

Opposite page: *Figs growing in a rain forest in Indonesia. They are plump and ripe—ready to become a hornbill's favorite meal.*

A Useful Tool

When it comes to eating, hornbills must be pleased to have such huge beaks. They are heavy birds, and much of the fruit they eat grows on branches that are too thin for them to perch on. The hornbill's long beak allows it to pluck distant fruit from the safety of a thick, sturdy branch.

Unlike most birds, hornbills have sharp ridges on the edges of their beaks. This means that they can tug fruit from branches without any fear of it slipping away from their grasp. It also allows them to bite chunks out of fruits that are too big to be swallowed whole.

When a hornbill swallows, it tosses its beak high in the air so that the food slides down its throat. However, if it is in a playful mood, it might throw the food high in the air and catch it on its way down!

A great hornbill delicately holds a fruit in its enormous beak, ready to swallow.

Deadly Hunters

Most hornbills eat animals in addition to fruit. They will make a meal out of anything small enough to catch. Their prey includes insects, lizards, small birds, rats, squirrels, and sometimes even snakes.

Eating meat is particularly important for hornbills that live in the savanna, where fruit is hard to find. African ground hornbills eat virtually nothing else. They spend their days walking slowly through the long grass, stopping occasionally to push over a stone or dig into the parched earth.

Hornbills in the savanna have many tricks for finding food. One of their favorites is to fly to the edge of a brushfire and catch small creatures as they flee from the flames. Some hornbills even work together with other animals when they hunt. Turn the page to learn about a remarkable friendship.

A ground hornbill eats a puff adder, using its long beak to keep the poisonous snake away from its face.

You Scratch My Back . . .

In parts of Africa hornbills have struck up an amazing friendship with the dwarf mongoose, a small but very fierce weasel-like creature. The mongoose and hornbill are so friendly that the hornbill will often wait by its partner's home in the morning and wake it up if it oversleeps!

The bird and beast go hunting together, with the mongoose leading the way and the hornbill flying behind. From its high position the hornbill can keep watch and warn the mongoose of any danger. This allows the mongoose to concentrate on the hunt. In return for its help the hornbill is allowed to pick off some of the lizards and grasshoppers that the mongoose disturbs.

In the African savanna a dwarf mongoose is a hornbill's best friend.

Whoosh!

A hornbill's wings are short, broad, and rounded. This is the perfect shape for bobbing and weaving through the jungle, where there are lots of obstacles, such as trees, to dodge.

Hornbills are strong fliers and can cover over seven miles (10 kilometers) without coming down to rest. They fly high above the forest, often taking energy-saving breaks from flapping by swooping and gliding instead. One species, the wreathed hornbill, crosses open seas every day as it travels from island to island.

Hornbills have holes in their wings. They are the only birds in the world with no underwing coverts—special feathers that cover up the gaps between the quills, or stems, of their long flight feathers. This means that with each flap of their wings the air rushing through the gaps makes a loud "whooshing" sound. This can be heard over half a mile (one kilometer) away and sounds exactly like the chuffing of an old locomotive.

Opposite page:
A male and female hornbill "whoosh" overhead like two locomotives in the sky!

Feather Care

The large feathers of a bird's wings and tail can easily be damaged in flight. Like all birds, hornbills have to spend a lot of time preening, or looking after, their feathers. They mend broken ones by combing and nibbling at them with their beaks, and they carefully reposition those that have been knocked out of place.

Like many birds, hornbills produce preen oil—a kind of bird shampoo—from special glands near their tails. By spreading this oil over their bodies, hornbills keep their feathers supple and waterproof.

Once a year a hornbill sheds, or molts, its feathers and grows a new set. With the exception of nesting mothers, who lose their feathers all at once, hornbills molt in stages. This means that they are always able to fly.

A red-billed hornbill preens itself to keep its feathers in top condition.

Bird Baths

Fleas and lice are a big problem for birds. Picking out these bugs from underneath their feathers is an important part of preening. The best way to stay bug-free, however, is to take lots of baths.

Although they never bathe in ponds or streams, hornbills often fly up to the top of the forest canopy after rain to rub themselves against the wet leaves. Afterward they stretch out their wings, spread their tails, fluff up their feathers, and bask in the sun until they are completely dry.

Another good way of killing off pesky bugs is dust bathing. To do this, a hornbill lies on the ground, stirs up dust with its feet, and spreads it all over its body with its wings.

After a good wash in the rain forest
a hornbill stretches out its feathers
to dry in the sunshine.

Keeping in Touch

Hornbills live in pairs, small family groups, or large flocks. They fly together, eat together, and, at the end of the day, sleep together. Their loud, booming voices are perfect for keeping in touch with one another in the dense rain forest, where it is often impossible to see farther than the next tree. Their calls also carry well over empty plains—the African ground hornbill's "hoo hoo hoo-hoo" can be heard over three miles (five kilometers) away.

Close up a hornbill can tell the age and sex of another member of its species by looking at its coloring, beak, and casque. Being able to guess another bird's age is very important, as young birds often follow the wise, experienced ones who are better at finding fruit trees.

Each year another wrinkle grows on this hornbill's casque. So count the wrinkles and you will know its age.

Roosting Together

Hornbills roost, or sleep, on high branches, hidden among the leaves. Most species sleep in the same place every night. Only the large ground hornbills do not—they cover such huge distances that going back to the same place would not be worth their while.

Roosting together reduces the hornbills' chances of being surprised by a predator such as an eagle or a big cat. Some species take great trouble to keep the whereabouts of their roosts secret. At dusk they crouch down in their usual sleeping position—with their bellies resting on their feet, their heads on their shoulders, and their beaks pointing up in the air. Then, as the last rays of sunlight fade, they fly off to a final, secret roosting site several hundred feet away.

In the savanna two hornbills roost in a thorn tree, protected from predators by the tree's thorns.

Plenty for Everyone

Although there are plenty of fig trees in the jungle, hornbills often have to fly for miles before they find one that is bearing fruit. They have to be quick, too, as within a few weeks a fruiting tree will have been stripped bare by local monkeys, insects, and other birds.

Because of this hornbills that eat a lot of fruit have to be good at working together. Some species roost in huge flocks of up to 100 birds. They fly in much smaller groups but keep in touch with other members of the flock by listening for each other's loud wing beats and calls. When a hornbill spots a fruiting tree, it is never long before the whole flock arrives to take a share in the pickings!

The bushy-crested hornbill does not have to rely on fruit for meals—it finds a centipede quite tasty, too.

It's All Mine!

Hornbills that live in the savanna also communicate with one another noisily, but for the opposite reason. To another member of its species a ground hornbill's booming call can mean only one thing: "Stay off my land!"

Rather than flying to and fro over a large area of forest, ground hornbills live in small family groups that "farm" a patch of savanna. If one group were to move onto another's territory, there might not be enough food to go around.

To mark their territories, hornbills of the savanna accompany their calls with a special dance or display. They spread their wing and tail feathers and wave their beaks in the air. If their warnings are ignored, hornbills are quite prepared to lash out with their long, sharp beaks. Ground hornbills that live near people often get into trouble for breaking windows— they mistake their own reflections for other birds intruding on their patch!

Opposite page:
A ground hornbill tries to intimidate intruders with an angry display of its feathers and a wave of its beak.

33

Loving Couples

Hornbills are at their noisiest in the nesting season. Even fruit-eating species that do not have feeding territories start displaying noisily in order to attract mates.

Hornbills that live in dry places breed only during the rainy season. This is when there is more food around, which is important as nesting is a difficult time for both parents and chicks. However, in rain forests it is warm and wet all year round, and hornbills can breed at any time.

Once a hornbill has found a mate, the pair stays together for life. The two birds fly together, preen each other's feathers, and even share food. In the nesting season male hornbills collect so much food for their families that the females never have to collect any for themselves.

Like all hornbill couples, these oriental pied hornbills will stay together for life.

Nesting

Hornbills nest in tree holes, but unlike woodpeckers, they cannot make their own. Instead they use large, natural holes that form when branches break off and the wood behind rots away.

Female hornbills spend a lot of time poking around searching for the perfect hole. To be safe from predators, a hole needs to be well hidden and high up from the ground, and it needs to have strong, thick walls. Inside it must be big and spacious, with a funk-hole, or chimney, for the mother and chicks to hide in if they are threatened.

Good holes are so hard to find that not all adult hornbills get the chance to breed during the nesting season. Those that find a good nesting hole often return to the same site year after year.

Shutting Up Shop

Once she has found the perfect hole, the female hornbill seals herself in using a mixture of mud, sticky fruits, and her own droppings. She leaves only a narrow slit in the center, just wide enough for her beak to poke through. The wall dries to become so hard that it can take her over a day to peck her way out.

Throughout the nesting period the mother keeps her eye pressed to the slit, watching for danger. If any creature comes too close, she stabs at it with her long beak from behind the rock-hard wall.

Sealing up the nest has another use as well. During the day the wall blocks out the sun and stops the nest from getting too hot. By the evening, however, the wall itself has become quite warm and heats up the nest during the cold night hours.

Helpless!

Once the nest has been sealed up, the female hornbill waits for several days or even weeks before laying her eggs. This is the final test of the male's ability to feed her—and later her chicks. If he is not up to the job, she breaks down the wall and flies away.

This might seem harsh, but what happens next really is a matter of life or death. As soon as she lays her eggs, the female hornbill starts molting her flight and tail feathers—not one at a time but all at once! This means that she will be unable to fly again until the eggs have hatched and the chicks are half-grown.

While the helpless female broods, or sits over, her eggs to keep them warm, the male spends all his time gathering food. When he comes back to the nest, he props himself up against the tree with his tail and passes his offerings through the slit.

The male hornbill passes food to the helpless female inside the nest hole.

Breaking Out

Opposite page:
After breaking out of her nest, this female hornbill has caught a gecko to feed to her chicks.

When the hornbill chicks hatch, they are blind, naked, and unable to stand up. They rely on their parents for everything. Within two days their skins fill up with air, giving them the look and feel of balloons! The air keeps them warm and helps stop them from bruising themselves on the floor of the nest.

By the time the chicks are strong enough to stand up and take food from the nest entrance, Mom has grown a new set of feathers. This means that she can break out of the nest to give Dad a helping hand. Once she has left, the chicks reseal the nest and start taking food from both parents.

Hornbills lay their eggs one after the other at intervals of between one and five days. This means that as the oldest chicks begin to break down the wall and leave the nest, the younger ones often try to seal the nest up again because they are not yet ready to go!

In the African savanna a young ground hornbill stays with its parents until it has learned to fly and find food for itself.

Free at Last!

When they finally break out of the nest, young hornbills are almost as big as their parents. Their beaks are smaller, however, and their casques have not yet begun to grow. They fly stiffly to nearby branches and stay close to the nest for a few days while they practice their flying skills.

At first the young birds are fed by their parents, but as time passes, young hornbills begin to hunt and search for fruit on their own. They learn many of the skills they will need as adults by watching their parents going about their daily tasks. The young hornbills have fun, too, playfighting and chasing each other around the branches at high speed.

In some species the young hornbills stay with their parents for years and help them to collect food for the next brood of chicks. The young birds need years of experience before they will be able to start families of their own.

Hornbills and People

Hornbills have always fascinated the people who live near them. For example, in parts of Africa people regard it as bad luck to see a hornbill on the ground. If they see one, they chase it until it takes off in fright.

In grassy savannas some huntsmen even disguise themselves as hornbills. They do this by wearing stuffed hornbill heads like hats and crouching down so that only the bird's head rises above the long grasses. Ground hornbills are also valued for their skill in hunting creatures that humans dislike, such as locusts, snakes, and scorpions.

Unfortunately the rainforest home of most hornbills is being cut down at an alarming rate. Unless people stop this destruction, many species of hornbills are certain to disappear.

Words to Know

Casque   The horny growth above the beaks of most hornbills.

Flock   A group of birds that fly, eat, or roost together.

Funk-hole   The "chimney" of a hornbill's tree hole. Hornbills hide in their funk-holes when their nests are attacked by creatures big enough to break down the protective walls.

Habitat   An animal's ideal natural environment.

Molting   Shedding old, worn-out fur or feathers in preparation for growing new fur or a new set of feathers.

Predator   An animal that hunts other animals for food.

Preening   Cleaning and repairing the feathers.

Rain forest   A dense tropical forest in an area of high rainfall. Rain forests are extremely rich in plant and animal life.

Roost   The place where a bird sleeps. When a bird sleeps, we say that it is roosting.

Savanna   A hot, grassy plain with little rainfall and few trees.

Territory   The area in which an animal hunts or breeds that is defended by the animal from intruders of its own species.

Underwing coverts   Feathers that cover up the gaps between the quills, or stems, of a bird's long flight feathers.

INDEX

Cover Photo: Anthony Bannister / NHPA
Photo Credits: Morten Strange / NHPA, pages 4, 20, 31, 35, 38; Anthony Bannister / NHPA, pages 7, 32; The Purcell Team / Corbis, page 8; Martin Harvey / NHPA, pages 11, 15, 27; Richard T. Nowitz / Corbis, page 12; Nigel J. Dennis / NHPA, pages 16, 23, 43; © Kennan Ward Photography / Corbis, page 19; Peter Lillie; ABPL / Corbis, page 24; Brian Vikander / Corbis, page 28; Sharna Balfour; ABPL / Corbis, page 40; Peter Johnson / © Corbis, page 44.